DISC
NASHVI

11/06

D1624379

JAN · 69

SOCKS *for* CHRISTMAS

ANDY ANDREWS

Rutledge Hill Press®
Nashville, Tennessee
A Division of Thomas Nelson Publishers
www.ThomasNelson.com

Photos on pages 4, 9, 12, 21, 23, 34, 49, 60 & 63 courtesy of the author.
Photos on pages 27 & 44 is courtesy of Laura Troup.
Photos of toys by Steve Gardner of Pixel Works.

Published by Rutledge Hill Press, a Division of Thomas Nelson, Inc.,
P.O. Box 141000, Nashville, Tennessee, 37214.

Rutledge Hill Press books may be purchased in bulk for educational, business, fundraising, or sales promotional use. For information, please e-mail SpecialMarkets@ThomasNelson.com.

1-4016-0239-8

Printed in the United States of America
05 06 07 08 09-5 4 3 2

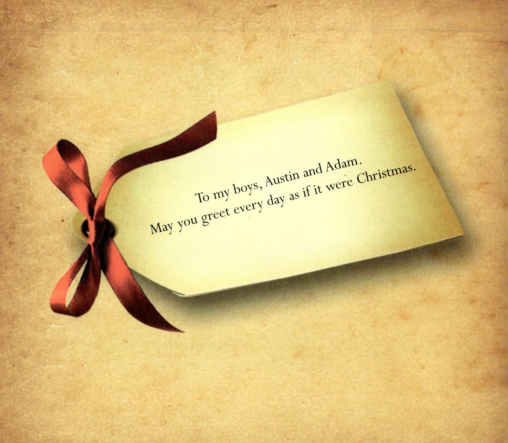

To my boys, Austin and Adam.
May you greet every day as if it were Christmas.

Acknowledgments

There are many people responsible for the publication of any book, and to all of you who have been involved in the publication of this one, the awe I have for your abilities and gratefulness for your efforts are paramount.

There are several people, however, without whom the story would never have been written. My parents, Joyce and Larry Andrews, who passed away when I was a young man, but not before teaching and showing me what Christmas was all about; my wife, Polly, who instills a Christmas spirit in our home the year-round; my manager and friend Robert D. Smith, who carries "Christmas morning" with him wherever he goes; and Danita Allen, my first editor. It is she who insisted the "Socks" story be written in the first place and managed to form a fledgling author's memories into a coherent manuscript. I cannot thank you enough for the guidance and encouragement.

T HERE ARE TWENTY-FOUR HOURS IN A DAY. Only twenty-four. That translates to 1,440 minutes or 86,400 seconds. Every single day of my adult life.

But as a boy, there was one night every year that lasted longer than any other—one night when clocks actually slowed down. This phenomenon generally occurred near the end of December, specifically the night of the twenty-fourth . . . Christmas Eve.

I had gone to bed at 9:00 P.M. after leaving a note, pound cake, and a glass of buttermilk for Santa Claus. Every Christmas Eve for as many of my ten years as I could remember that's what I left him: a note, pound cake, and a glass of buttermilk.

The note contained the usual niceties about being careful not to slip on the roof and saying hello to Rudolph, but its primary purpose was, of course, to make one last stab at getting the presents I wanted. The pound cake was left over from Jesus' birthday party, which we had celebrated before bedtime, and the buttermilk . . . well, the buttermilk was always left because my dad insisted that it was Santa's favorite drink. Personally, I hated the stuff, but since my father drank it by the gallon, I assumed he knew.

By 10:30 I was still awake. I was mentally tracing Santa's route to our house at 1505 Randal Road. It did concern me somewhat that he might not find me because of a mistake on the road signs. Randal at one end of our road was spelled with one L, and at the other end, the sign proclaimed Randall with two Ls.

Would he be able to locate me? Maybe he would get confused, come in from Randal Road once, and later enter the neighborhood by way of Randall Road, and I'd get presents twice. Not likely, I knew, but these are the kinds of things a kid thinks about on Christmas Eve.

Earlier I had heard on the local news that Santa's sleigh had been tracked on radar leaving Thailand, and the predictions were that he would soon be in Singapore. I wasn't sure where Singapore was, but I thought it might be near Mississippi, which was the state next to us. In any case, that's why I went to bed at 9:00.

Eleven o'clock. I wasn't even sleepy. I could smell the Christmas tree from the bedroom. My dad loved Christmas and would have had our tree up, trimmed, and glowing by Labor Day if my mom had let him; but as she told him every year, our family was not going to skip Thanksgiving.

As it was, the tree had been decorated since the day after Thanksgiving and would remain so until a loud discussion occurred between my parents. This discussion usually took place around the first of February. Although my mother consistently prevailed and the tree did come down, I always thought my dad had a strong argument by pointing out that just because the needles had fallen off the tree, that didn't necessarily mean it was dead.

The tree itself stretched fifty feet in the air. The fact that we only had an eight-foot ceiling casts a shadow of doubt on my recollection of this particular point, but you get the idea—it was a big tree!

We bought a blue spruce every year. That variety was, according to my dad, the only real Christmas tree. A blue spruce was more aromatic, was the same kind of tree Jesus had as a boy, and, he explained, wouldn't get sap all over the carpet like "a stinkin' Scotch pine"!

Family tradition dictated that we make our own decorations. Though the tree looked beautiful to me, in reality, it was probably kind of junky. Construction paper chains, stars shaped out of pipe cleaners, and bells made from foil covered Dixie Cups were everywhere. I hung a toilet brush from the bathroom on it one year, and no one noticed it for days.

At 12:01 A.M. it was technically Christmas, but I knew better than to venture into the living room. I was to stay in bed until Mom and Dad came to get me—besides, I didn't want to blow the whole deal. I had been warned repeatedly that Santa would not come until I was asleep.

But how was I supposed to go to sleep? This was only the most incredible day of the year. There was no way I could go to sleep! I'd have to fake it and just hope Santa wasn't as sharp as everyone said. No way was I going to sleep. I just wouldn't! Heck, I'd already been awake for a week. I'd just stick it out till daylight.

"Son? Son!" My father shook me. I opened my eyes.

"Santa . . . ," he said, "has been here!"

Ignoring the fact that I had indeed gone to sleep, I jumped out of bed and ran to the living room. The tree (more than one hundred feet tall now) was almost covered with gifts and toys of every sort. There was the basketball I'd asked for! Where was the BB gun? There was the Incredible Edible Machine—now I could make bugs to eat in front of my sister! Where was my BB gun? Ah, my Candyland game! Baseball glove! G. I. Joe! My BB gun must be one of the wrapped presents!

But it wasn't. Neither was the electric football game I'd wanted. I did, however, get two sweaters, blue jeans, a white belt, and from my Aunt Ruth . . . socks.

Socks! Who wanted socks? What kind of Christmas present was socks? I had socks. I had a drawer full of socks. I was not pleased.

All in all, however, my haul was impressive. I had scored on some of the main things I'd wanted, and if I didn't think about the clothes and especially the socks, I was happy.

Before too long, the most important part of Christmas was at hand. My dad was asleep in the recliner, Mom was in the kitchen, and I was now free to compare loot with my friends.

This ritual, practiced by every kid since time began, was a large part of our growing up process. Ten years old seems a little early to be concerned with "keeping up with the Joneses," but that's exactly what we did.

My first stop was two houses down. Johnny Hamilton had gotten a bicycle. It had a tiger-striped banana seat and spider handlebars. It was beautiful, but he wouldn't let me ride it, so I left. Later that day, while showing off for Cathy Burns, Johnny tried to pop a wheelie, fell off the bike, and cried. I laughed.

Down the street, Greg and Richard Fraley were in the guinea pig business. Mr. Fraley had made a trip to the emergency room early that morning after being bitten by the one named Charley. He hated those guinea pigs after that, but he never again tried to put a bow on one.

Roger Loften had gotten the electric football game I had wanted. Graciously pointing out the flaws in that particular model, I generally acted unimpressed. Roger had also received the Rock 'em Sock 'em Robots. We didn't play with them because, thanks to his brother Stuart, they were already broken.

Danny Foster's dad was a doctor. They lived across Cherokee Avenue in another, much nicer neighborhood. I hated going to Danny's house that morning. I knew what Danny had gotten for Christmas—everything! He had an Operation game, Battleship, a tetherball set, the deluxe model electric football game, a real minibike (four horsepower), a bicycle like Johnny's (only better), a trampoline, a swing set . . . and a BB gun!

I stayed at Danny's house for more than an hour. Danny really knew how to show a kid a good time. We dug a hole in the vacant lot next door and put the box from the trampoline over it. Great fort!

Walking home, I was imagining Christmas dinner. I felt sure that we'd have the same wonderful menu that we'd had the year before: turkey and dressing with cranberry sauce, sweet potato casserole (with pecans and brown sugar on top), peas, corn, pickled peaches, and homemade rolls. I walked faster.

Rounding the corner behind the Vine and Olive Motel, I saw Timmy Johnson and his sister, Barbara, tossing an old tennis ball in their front yard. As usual, neither was wearing a jacket, though the temperature was in the forties. Timmy was in my class at school; Barbara was three years older.

They didn't seem to have many friends. Even at lunchtime they would go out on the playground to swing from the jungle gym or just talk. They never went with us into the cafeteria and never brought a sack lunch. The Loften boys said it was because they were snobs. I thought maybe so too.

"Hi, Timmy," I said as I approached. "What'd ya get for Christmas? I got everything I wanted except a BB gun and an electric football game."

They continued tossing the ball. Back and forth. Thinking he didn't hear me, I tried again. "Hey! Show me what you got for Christmas!"

JAN • 69

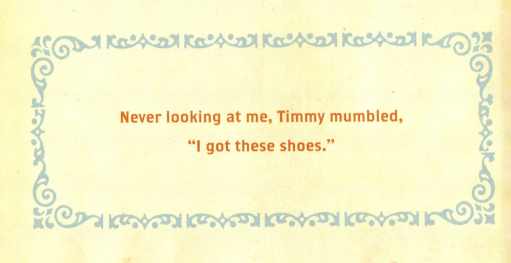

Never looking at me, Timmy mumbled,

"I got these shoes."

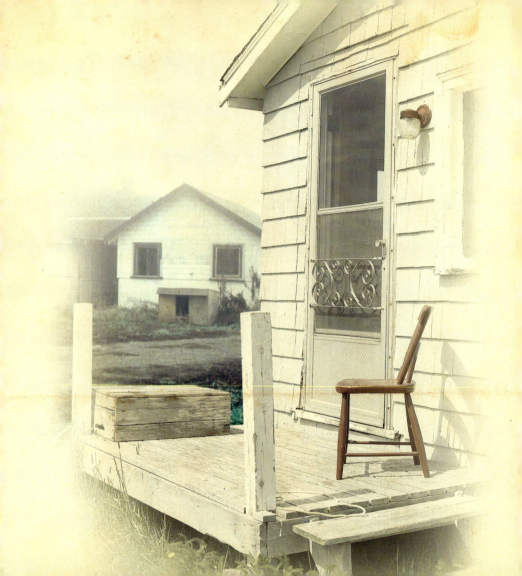

I could see the shoes he had received. Big, black, hard leather shoes that looked as if they might belong to my grandfather. But they were shined, polished, and tied directly onto his feet. Barbara had on a pair that didn't appear to be drastically different.

I had never seen either of them with anything other than tennis shoes. Once, Timmy was sent home from school for showing up barefooted. After that, he was absent for a week.

Watching them continue to throw the ball, I noticed something not quite right. I said, "That's not the way you're supposed to wear those shoes."

The ball fell to the ground. As they turned to face me, Barbara said, "What do you mean by that? We're wearing them just like you are—on our feet!"

She looked mad. I tried to explain myself. "Yeah, that's right," I stammered, "but you're not wearing socks. You're supposed to wear socks with those kinds of shoes."

For a moment we stared at each other. Then, without warning, Timmy started crying and ran inside. Barbara called me a name and ran after him. I stood there a few minutes wondering what I had done. I even knocked on their door. No one answered, so I went home.

When I arrived home, I told my parents what had happened with Timmy and Barbara. I told them exactly what I'd said. My mom had tears running down her cheeks as my dad picked me up and carried me to my bedroom. I thought I was about to get a spanking, but instead, he hugged me.

He told me all about why Danny Foster got big presents and why I didn't get an electric football game. Gently, he explained to me about Santa Claus and buttermilk. And then, wiping the tears from my face, he told me why my friends didn't wear socks with their shoes.

I now remember that day as an awakening. I had never known there were families without enough to eat. Amid all the decorations and songs and parties surrounding our most magical holiday, it had never occurred to me that some parents might do without the luxury of socks for their children simply because they couldn't afford them.

JAN • 69

Many holiday seasons have passed since that year. Timmy and Barbara moved away while I was in the fourth grade. I never saw them again, but I have never forgotten that Christmas. Wherever I live there will always be people in my own neighborhood who are, in some way, less fortunate than I.

And to this day, there is one Christmas gift I treasure above all others—the gift of a pair of socks.

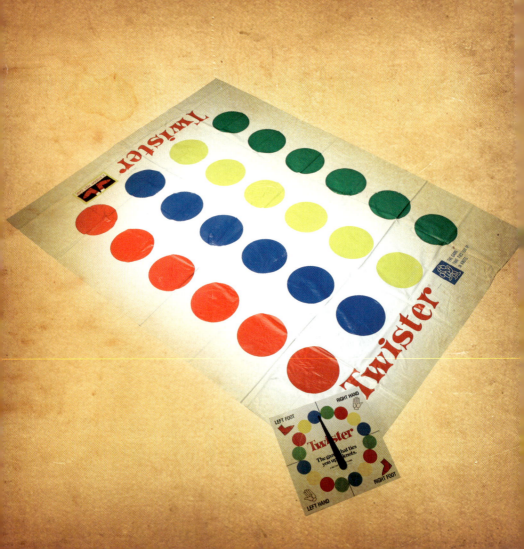

I<small>F YOU LIKE</small> *Socks for Christmas*
A<small>ND WANT TO READ MORE PLEASE VISIT:</small>

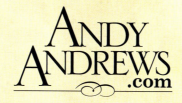